Sentiments

c a gallagher

 gallchobhair publishing

2015

© 2015 by c. a. gallagher and Gallcobhair Publishing, Inc.

All Rights Reserved. Except as permitted under the U.S. Copyright Act of 1976 or for the use of brief quotations in a book review or scholarly journal, no part of this publication may be reproduced, distributed, set to music, or transmitted in any form or by any means, or stored in a database or retrieval system, without the prior written permission of the author or publisher.

Gallchobhair Publishing
2850 Dupont Commerce Ct.
Fort Wayne, IN 46845

The Gallcobhair Publishing Logo is trademark of Gallcobhair Publishing Company.

First Edition: October 2015
ISBN-10: 0692558772
ISBN-13: 978-0-692-55877-5

Ordering Information:
Special discounts are available on quantity purchases by corporations, associations, educators, and others. For details, contact the publisher at the address above.

U.S. trade bookstores and wholesalers: Please contact Gallchobhair Publishing Company - Tel: (775) 219-2996.

On the Covers:
The cover art (front & back) is a digital print of a high-resolution photograph of the oil painting by c a gallagher entitled "Channel Lights."

The print and the high-resolution photograph are © 2012-2015 by c. a. gallagher. All Rights Reserved. The image was taken on a Nikon 2000 film camera. A printed copy of the image was scanned into a JPEG image via an Epson WF-7610 All-in-One Printer.

"Channel Lights" is a 30" H x 40" W oil painting. The original canvas enjoys a marvelous exposure over a glorious fireplace in an elegant home in Savannah, Georgia.

Dedication

These words & ideas are dedicated to my much loved muse, Jacqueline Taylor-Scott, for all her caring and support.

Beloved wife, lover & companion; my best friend!

Without your support and patience, I would have never achieved my dream.

Contents

Foreword i
Acknowledgements iii
Special Dedication iv
a new year's sentiments 1
brilliant presence 2
do you watch too? 3
the dance eclectic 4
and we anew 5
smile within, without 6
yes 7
each time 8
slippery, silent echo 9
two loves 11
... and 12
the dance anew 13
wondrous events 14
gravitas 15
the benign prerogative 16
mea culpa 17
a change is gonna come 18
legacy 19
can we 20
darling lady 21
the edge 22
thoughts 23
fireside one 24
father and son 25
dream state 26
cold mask of winter 27
a thought, too 28
promise of spring 29

would you believe	30
just saw a dream	31
breath of the mountain	32
dance of the two lips	33
lucky one he	34
together	35
to the green	36
approval	37
return renewed	38
it falls apart	39
hills of michigan	40
nostalgia	41
too far	42
avant-garde and kitsch	43
lawrence	44
mankind	45
cumberbatch & armitage	46
ashley	48
i'm not paralyzed	49
land of the dead?!	50
escarpment of neverland	51
she dances	52
the canvas	53
at the end of the driveway	54
nici	55
sea quest I	56
sea quest I	56
sea quest II	57
sea quest III	58
sea quest IV	59
tomfoolery & shenanigans	60

you loved me once	61
granddad's dirt	62
sweet	67
fan dance – an abstraction	69
smoke, no mirrors – an interpretation	71
optical haiku	73
metallica	75
ink blots	77
lovers?	79
garden of the mind	81
the song fades away	85
wake up, little susie	86
... & did we pass?	87
acclaimed, but troubled	89
actor of depth	90
maya	92
maya, too	93
gone, but not	94

Foreword

I have led a most interesting life; from poverty to riches and back again. Here I sit, laptop on my lap (whodda thunk it!), trapped within four small walls of a hotel room - not by choice, but necessity, and unfortunately, my family is trapped here with me. Of course it could be worse, We could be totally homeless like so many of my Viet Nam Veteran brothers are.

I am trying desperately to regain some semblance of order to my life and, as in times past, I turn to my arts for solace, clarity of mind and vision. I have great hopes of somehow getting a new collection of three books of poetry: "Sentiments," "In Memoriam - 2014, Part 1," and my book of artwork and poetry - "the tenor of image" - published before the end of this year. Samples of "the tenor of image" and " In Memoriam" are included in the back of this book

I remember distinctly the first day that I sat down to put to paper from pen, words, thoughts and sentiments. I was 14 and in the hospital suffering from ulcer's; I know, WAY too young, but such is the penalty of a 140 IQ at that age and realizing that you were the mental giant in your family and that they would NEVER understand you, and were, quite possibly, slightly afraid of you. While in the hospital, my best friend in the world, Manny (he still is, God bless him!) brought me some volumes of prose & poetry from the library. I devoured volumes from Jack Kerouac, Lawrence Ferlinghetti, and e. e. cummings during my hospital stay and over the rest of the summer. The words of these Masters drove me to explore my own voice.

The first attempts weren't very good I admit, but with much wrestling and thousands of attempts I began to flourish on my own.; began to find a voice.

I received acclaim from my English teachers for my prose and poetry throughout the 8th through 11th grades. But it was my 10th through 12th grade Art teacher - Mrs. Dorothy (Dottie) Kennedy, the single greatest influence on my life as an artist, that turned the corner for me. She insisted that I write on a daily basis and that I turn in the work I had put in every Friday. There were several times when I had a work of fiction, one or two volumes of poetry, a drama, and several artworks all in stages of completion during a single week. It was one of the greatest flourishes of artistic expression in my lifetime.

Her influence extended not only to my poetry, but my painting, mixed media artwork, writing, and even sculpting. Under her tutelage, I had several major one man art shows, sold artwork to influential homes and businesses (two banks, several real estate companies, and some small shops) throughout Florida. I also sold to other students and their parents. My brother recently reminded me that I sold a clay sculpture of a horse's head to one of Mrs. Kennedy's friends who had seen it sitting at her house awaiting a grade. He paid me $500 for the piece, which in 1967 was a princely sum of money; especially to someone whose family didn't see much more than $500 during a month.

My poetry tends to ramble through a wide variety of styles, images, thoughts and sentiments. I try NOT to pigeon hole them, nor try to bind them into one group, but rather let them roam free and clear to end where they may. This collection of works marks this landscape. For me, this, and the other books in this small collection, are a labor of love and passion; a bit of mental solace and stimulation. I hope you enjoy reading it as much as I did writing it!

Acknowledgements

As already stated, I owe much to the literary styling's of Jack Kerouac, Lawrence Ferlinghetti, and e. e. cummings.

I also owe much to the training, caring, and pushing provided by Dottie Kennedy. I miss you dear, and probably never told you how much you did for me, or how much you meant to me.

I also owe a lot to the "other" woman in my life that provided guidance, support and encouragement throughout my entire life regardless of the endeavor, my dear Mother, Helen Gallagher whose last name I use as my Nom de Guerre (for my artwork), and also as my Nom de Plume for my poetry and fictional writing.

Special Dedication

Prior to the publication of this book of poetry, my very special force behind my sails, my beloved Mother, passed away. She went to join her Father, my Grandfather William Gallagher, and my much loved son, Cristofer Lee Scott, a great buddy poet in his own right.

To say that I miss her is a mere understatement. She was the "wind beneath my wings" for all of my life. I find myself reaching for the phone to call her as I did nearly every day for over 30 years. Doing even the most mundane of things during the day brings thoughts of her to mind, and I find myself delving into tears and memories.

There are many poems within these pages that are dedicated to her or her memory. I won't list them here; rather, I will let you enjoy the journey of discovering them for yourselves.

As always, my dearest readers, comments, criticisms, critiques, and just good humor can be sent my way via:
  mailto:cagallagher@cagallagher.com or
mailto:cagallagher@cagallaghergallery.com.

Sentiments

a new year's sentiments

   i reflect these wishes
to you & yours,
   may the New Year' be in keeping
with grandiose cosmotic events,
   and your life be
moved toward fulfillment.

brilliant presence

what is this brilliant presence?
    she asked, demurely, eyes
    wondrous, trusting,
is it my beauty?
    coyly batting an eye and smiling,
    aye, for you are most fair of face ... but,
is it my lithe and supple body?
    preening, posing, and teasing,
    you are both delightful to behold, and hold ... but,
is it my hair, my eyes?
    frustration now growing, yet
    curious still,
    hair & eyes the color of earth, beautiful ... but,
what is my brilliant presence, then?
    hurt, confused, but wondering,
    hoping,
    'tis all of these, yet more,
    you glide thru space, not shifting or molding,
    purely passing,
    when you smile, the day is dazzled,
    when you are near me, my heart dances,
    moreover, in my arms, you are all that makes
    my world right!

do you watch too?

dance the flowers whose
billowing seeds spread
hither and yon – floating away;
the dreamscape watcheth,
and i,
ever mindful of its presence,
escape the cosmotic gaze,
hidden well within –
peeking out only
to validate my own existence,
hah!
i see me –
just in & thru
your eyes –
do you watch too?

the dance eclectic

derive your ideals, your style,
your taste from
    a diverse range of sources,
set them wide-ranging,
broad-based, being extensive
    & comprehensive
is key,
choose them wisely
from the all–pervading jungle,
do not follow
    any one system,
    nor philosophy,
but select, then use,
    the best of essentials,
forge your dance,
noting works of architecture,
ideas of decoration, then
base your life on historic styles,
chosen for their fancy appropriateness
    to tradition,
whirl – like a dervish – to the dance,
the dance eclectic.

and we anew

it's about death, and life,
of love & being, of caring & seeing,
of memories,
my mother and father dancing together,
my daughters first step,
my son's death &
    the lingering grief,
    a pain that may diminish
        but never die,
the day my father died,
    the joy of my mom still with me,
the day she no longer will,
yet i renew a new song,
my song, and i've cried
    & laughed & loved & lived,
and i find myself in love again, the last love,
and we anew
    bring a solace to living
      & loving & kissing &
    i love you this big,
    this much, this hard, this long
as we anew, continue my song.

smile within, without

there are smiles with eyes,
  with heart,
  with lip, and then
there are smiles that
  permeate the air,
give breathe of life,
radiate warmth & dispel despair
smiles whose being seems
  simply to exist,
the chesire cat would be proud!

Sentiments

yes

yes, you are all that,
beautiful,   fair of face,
an entrancing vision
*   to all who observe, and*
yes, i am one of those,
one who watches,   appreciates, even
*   dreams of becoming involved*
*   with beauty such as yours,*
deep and true and pure, and yes,
*   like those other hopefuls,*
i dream and wish to know you,
know the true essence of you, and
yes, also like those others,
i approve of, enjoy, am rapt with appreciation
of the you glimpsed only from afar,
surreal, and so, i allow myself to voice
these idylls only through my pen,
such is the way of life,
*   so close, yet so far,*
alas, such can be this world.

each time

each time i pass a furtive glance
deep into your eyes, i cringe –
just a little, for those eyes bewitch &
drive to fore, the buried dreams,
held deep within.
images of dancing close, holding my love tightly,
cheek brushing cheek, breath drawing breath,
a warm embrace – shared,
yet – even faced with that ever-so-light twinge
the embrace causes,
i cannot refuse to look at you,
speak with you, plan with you,
for to do so would deny me, and these
feelings that desire so much to run rampant,
yet, i hold in check.
but — each glance, each smile,
each simple chance meeting of our eyes,
provides depth to these desires
and draws them one step closer
to reality!

slippery, silent echo

there was this dream i formed, long ago,
an empty reflection of what, i didn't know,
i never knew it was present, or even existed
'til the sight of you, brought it home.
so now i wonder, will I ever know
what i've been missing? the simple, tasty pleasure,
of you and i kissing,
of passions yielding to your charms,
or the calm, silent solace, of lying in your arms.
one slippery, silent echo, in my empty heart,
one slippery, silent echo, streaming tears a' start,
just one slippery, silent echo away.
though deeply hidden once, the dreams are back,
needing only encouragement to get them on track,
like an undernourished newborn,
lying delicate and light,
till the slightest whisper from you, gave them life.
so now will I know what my life's been missing?
or will this dream die a piteous thing?
stranded here in deepening light, once again safe
in the sweet soft cushion of night.
one slippery, silent echo, in my empty heart,
one slippery, silent echo, streaming tears a' start,
just one slippery, silent echo away.
this vision, once of promise, now withered on vine,
lay safe while unbidden, lost when no longer mine,
now it hides, in the shadows in shriveled up fear,
letting no one else close, letting no one else near,
one slippery, silent echo, in my empty heart,
one slippery, silent echo, streaming tears a' start,
just one slippery, silent echo away.
i hope never now to guess what the fuss was,
nor understand just what the mess was,
for you've given that dream a mild little tweak,
made it wake up and listen, made it speak,
so now will I know, what my life's been missing?
or will this dream die a piteous thing?

*stranded here again in deepening light,
once again safe in the cushion of night.
one slippery, silent echo, in my empty heart,
one slippery, silent echo, streaming tears a' start,
just one slippery, silent echo away*

two loves

two loves exist, from which to choose,
with one you win, the other lose,
one is Rich & Grand & Hot,
the other Safe & Sane & Not,
so which to choose?
i answer one,
for Safe is for those with rest in mind,
and Sane? Oh my - you jest - so kind,
and Not, Not you say,
Not Hot?
for me
i'll take the burning kind,
for Rich is the life touched by passions flame,
and Grand the memories lit by same,
and as for Hot, i tell you now,
those not scorched by loves sweet pain,
find little solace,
in summer rain!

... and

... and in your arms,
passion lies quietly,
awaiting but a simple whisper;
when the brush of soft lips
grasps my breath,
rending it
from my body,
flinging it outward
to explode
in raw,
impassioned beauty,
to dance with ...
to rival ...
the stars!

the dance anew

a love song
    relating to different times
but a tribute always to love & understanding,
    to pride & glory,
    to sense & sensibility,
to those we love
both in the here & now,
    and those now passed,
to be right with God for only He knows
the time you have with those
whose hearts are yours,
for none are promised tomorrow,
nor the next breath
thank God, or fate, or the heavenly cosmos
for each breath you take,
each step,   each waking moment,
able to be with those you love,
and provide for them   as best you can,
all the while avoiding the dirt nap two-step,
the dance of life,
the dance anew!

wondrous events

*a soft wind sighs
in the wake of your passing,
carrying aloft the scent
that implants firmly,
the vision of you
that lies burned onto closed eyelids;
adrift, not quite sleeping,
but resting in the warm cocoon of
between,
this image stays and
promises wondrous events,
upon your return.*

gravitas

a bullfight with gravity,
this silent fall from grace,
a simple stumble against
the raging rock of inspiration,
the spiritual haiku of moonlight,
the dancing promise of sun mites
'cross a golden meadow,

a tussle with chaotic forces,
with promises made and trampled,
dreams trashed, thrown out like
so much cosmic garbage, to be shuffled
& shunted amongst stardust, celestial debris
awaiting the crash & burn of id,
self-effacing aggrandizing, until the plaque sets in,

you want a piece of me?
you tumultuous flow of time?
you turbulent passage of ages?
i'm right here, come on; take the piece
if you can, take your best shot
cause i am still standing and
don't worry, i will remain so,

to the bitter end! *gravitas!*

the benign prerogative

truly a bag of dynamite,
explosive, controversial, a frozen hell,
a volatile confluence
of choice, of sanction, of privilege,
a cosmic dance with visions & comets,
    hardly are there words
especially from one who lives them,
and i'm feeling alright, mostly,
anticipatory, sure, but excited, mostly,
but, it is my prerogative,
    benign though it be!

mea culpa

mea culpa – acknowledgement,
i screwed up, i failed, i did it.

i went and fell in love
will the all that is you.

go ahead, shoot me, it's
my fault, go ahead and blame me!

but, who can fault me? look
at you, see who you are,

beauty & grace, so fair of face
& form, a delight to the senses,

and i, as many others before are
captured by the spell that is

the essence of you – mea culpa!

a change is gonna come

is it welcome, this
pending change?
this penchant for over statement
over achieving, over simplifying?
and we know with certitude
that it's coming,

but what does it mean?
what does it portend,
this transformation? this sally
into the unknowable, the unforeseen?
hope, promise, unexpected potential
and it's coming.

Sentiments

legacy

does what is done now impact
that which is left at last behind?
is there a legacy, do i care?
a man of conviction,
or convenience?
full of self loathing, or purely
self abnegation?

nietzsche wrote of the genealogy
of morals in which he provided
analysis of good, bad, and evil,
pollock & rothko, newmann &
still expanded our abstraction,
cummings, maya, & frost lead our
minds out of delusion,

often, strength and action are replaced
by passivity and nihilism, leading our
origins of guilt, and punishment, our
concept of justice, should we dissect
the meaning of our ascetic ideals?
should our certainty , our confidence,
our conviction be ruled by disbelief?

can we

can we find our truth, our way
back up the roads both well & less traveled?
shall we dance the golden, dappled
meadows of our youth?
do we relive adolescent glories, or
childlike exuberances?

can we once again capture those lost
treasures of childhood long shrouded
by misty fogs of delight?
or are we doomed to revel in shadows,
mere reflections of long ago that
linger still as aged photographs of
what was?

can we resolve, can we?

darling lady

*it was grand to find you here again
where once i left you,
pages in hand,
for i feared i might never have occasion
to put to paper, from pen,
words inspired by truth,
images haunted still, by
the beauty of you;*

*yet, here you are,
much to my
surprise and elation,
still available to receive
the ramblings of my silent, still observation
placed as they are,
flowing without so much
as a by-your-leave, flowing
here, to you from me;*

*so, as in times past,
i thank you
heartily for the chance
to chase my muse.*

the edge

it's silent protection, this chilly gaze,
slipped into eyes once warm
      now ablaze with warning echoes
      of fear and passion and pain,
remembrances of hurts just passed and the
      pretense of knowing & not caring,

holding you off at arm's length - the edge
    a hurtin' heart needs!

i hide behind haunted eyes, and yes,
i flinch at touches tender, for
      i remember how quickly departed
      the touches were, and the hurt
echoes of empty arms remembered - the past
      building high, again and again,

the wall that is that saving grace - the edge
a hurtin' heart needs!

thoughts

i wonder and conjecture, face this meeting
with trepidation —
for our meeting was rare, fortunate,
      yet ... still i feel somehow electric,
        somehow taken by the suddenness,
timeliness of this touch on soul and heart,

i sense, am afraid, yes ... even scared,
apprehensive —
for you have taken me aback,
      with your approach, the sheer
      knowledge, dare i say ... hope,
as if i know you already in some esoteric way,

i dwell, on familiarity with that
which seems,
on retrospective view, to be
      you, alas, it seems it may
      be this familiarity i fear,
but, as ever far braver souls before me have done,

i forge my way into this new wonderful vastness,
a brave new explorer, leading with chin
and a ... 'lead on, MacDuff',
'DAMN the torpedoes, full speed head',

fireside one

i, misty eyed, thoughtful,
    wrapped in the soft,
      sweet shawl of memory,
sit and drink my cinnamon cider,
toasting by the fire,
warm in the reverie,
    the vision,
remembered touch, smell
    of you
so recent in my arms,
so light against my shoulder
        as there you lie,
dreaming with the dances of the flames,
not these same, but those past,
and i am comforted,
    for as long as you lie there,
i am content.

father and son

    and here, the deep hidden past comes
back to niggle at my heart & mind,
for as i watch with trepidation, the
metaphors of war, listening to
haunting strains & lilting voice
          sing of loss,
             for as those images creep by
        my heart & mind, my aching thoughts
spin back to the day of my father's
flagged draped coffin, and
that overwhelming grief,
 that heart wrenching pain
where tears unbidden,   stream –
never, in my wildest nightmares,
was the depth of that pain & grief expected   to
double down the years to fall at the feet
      of another memory, another coffin,
not flag draped, but even more painful,
too much for one to live through,
      father and son, losses too huge to bear,
yet i do, i know not how, pain and loss,
      too much, too much,
father and son!

dream state

    cool side of the pillow,
    consort of REM,
    harbinger of fantasy –
    momentum - inertia-less
            travel to
            worlds of wonder
                    'neath stars alight,
            cosmic fires
                    that dream & dance
                fairy light –
Mona Lisa smile,
the countenance of one
        who sleeps on
the cool side of the pillow!

cold mask of winter

when you pull back the wintry sky
and gaze upon the mountains winter face
you find the anguished meadow
hiding 'neath its snowy mask,
and the seeds of spring nestled
quiet & serene, simply awaiting
the warming breath of spring
to burst forth in glorious union
saluting the sun!

and we wait, with quiet anticipation,
the chance to once again sing of springs rebirth,
and the promise of hearts , aflame with desire,
for like the nestled seed, hearts that lost
in the cold, dark doldrums of winter,
await the wakening promised
with springs warming rain, and love,
like those sprouting seeds, awaits
the sun's nourishment!

i am one of those, lost in dark winters night,
where love was rent asunder, the promise lost,
the desperate air sucked out of the room,
my life spiraling in the deepening gloom
darkening my mood, my thoughts, my hope,
but slowly the gloom has lightened,
and like the slumbering spring,
waits to reawaken to the warmth
of new dreams!

ah, new hopes, a new heart & new love,
the blood quickens with anticipation!

a thought, too

regret not those things undone,
                nor regret those once done,
learn, and go on,
for if you let fester those regrets
into your decrepitude,
you will miss the beauty of that
not yet found.

promise of spring

springtime in the Rockies,
face the mountain's fresh breath
as it wafts down
      the hillside newly green,
life awakening to fluff & preen,
refreshing long silent limbs,
watch the frolicking regeneration
      life springing hope anew,
for here is our hopes rejoined,
to realize there is more to life
than bitterness and pain,
      like love & joy,
for such is the promise of
springtime in the Rockies,
a gamboling, frolicking start anew,
      and the hope of finding
another you! come springtime,
refresh the promise, refresh my soul,
reveal the secrets, send the breath of
      love's freedom, let it come & stay!

would you believe

a pathetic silhouette,
lost and alone in a land without heart,
so sits this mere shade of man,
hidden in the depths and shadows of his realm,

would you believe
a previous social butterfly, sits dejected
and shattered? an empathetic epithet,
abandoned as planned to once again start,

an initiate with a plan,
still hidden, yet seeking the light from which
to emerge, escape from the darkness
the first step to overwhelm?

the city is my oubliette,
escape my ultimate goal
    for renewed love!

just saw a dream

what a wondrous moment,
what a bizarre little scheme,
the cosmos would tease with,
just saw a dream!
she waltzed so unaware,
as if from a long lost dream,
like a queen of my night,
a cosmic theme!
could she be   my waking daydream?
a beautiful sight,   a moonbeam?
                                     my unrest to foment?
cosmos, is that what you deem?
to add she to my kith?
just saw a dream!
can i try, do i dare, is it as simple as it seems?
shall we dance the sun bright,
with waltzing moon mites scheme?
could she be   my waking daydream?
a beautiful sight,   a moonbeam?
                                     my unrest to foment?
just saw a dream!

breath of the mountain

gossamer - delicate, sheer, and filmy,
breath of the mountain
    fresh & blowing
clearing away the mists
    of depression, of regret,

ethereal - fragile, frail, and pleasant,
whisper of wind blow, clear my way
    to love, new life,
chase away the old dreams,
    old schemes, old life,

sweetly - like the mountain's
freshening breath, my new
dream has waltzed into view
    and i believe anew,
that love can be found,
    for one who has lost!

dance of the two lips

*was that a smirk? a smile? what
twist of that sweet, luscious pair
    shown on me
the dance that lights, the dance that delights,
the prize striven for with each furtive glance,
there it is, the two-lip dance.*

*was that a frown? a grimace? no?
but something displayed there,
    shared between we,
enhancing our nights, teasing our knights,
the prize striven for with each furtive glance,
there it is, the two-lip dance.*

*was that a tease? a taunt? what
emotion, what passion, where
    else would it be,
what simple flights of fancy pledged, what sights
upon the countenance prance,
the promise of the two-lip dance!*

lucky one he

were that I were,
that lucky one he,
meant for a lifetime,
with this wondrous she,

to travel the world,
        travel the stars,
sweet talk the moon,
        capture ol' Mars,

wrap it all up,
as a present for she,
a simple love token,
from this besotted he,

for wondrous would
this life of mine be,
were that i were,
that lucky one he!

together

end of hard times,
feel i can't go on, for down
is the direction i flow on my own
so, maybe we can end the hard times,
launch the coming good times,
for now i can't imagine no you,
together, from one to we,
end of hard times, start of good times,
together, i look forward to
the loving times we'll go thru,
fresh beginnings flow, not alone,
so, maybe you'll find what's sweet
about me, and i'll get to discover
what's sweet about you,
together, from one to we,
end of hard times, start of good times,
together.

to the green

our chance to follow the sun,
    fly to the green,
no, not the emerald isle,
but the intensity, power -
a world away from our
    mountain eyrie,

and i, with my new one
    hand in hand,
bouncing down the aisle
minute by minute, hour
by heart skipping hour
    tired, but not weary,

for we start our new affair
    flying to the green,
our private emerald isle
celebrating hopes that soar
high as our mountain tor
    mountain eyrie,

and we two travel anew,
flying to the green.

approval

    since you want to know,
    he has been there thru all
    that's good and all that's bad
    my whole life thru,
    he's my best friend and
    the only approval
    i need, or will pursue,
    my daughter and my boy,
    have voices, true,
    but his is the only approval,
                    i need of you.

    he is a mirror of the me
    i have always wanted to be
    and a true reflection
    of the desires
    my empty life requires
    and every approval i didn't pursue
    collapsed,
    not what is wanted for you,
    nor needed to complete my new
    life moving forward, an approval
                  for you!

return renewed

paper thin wisps,
fireworks on display
shooting across the evening sky -
    a salute to a glorious end
to a salubrious day,

a fitting end to a romantic
get away - we are renewed
relaxed, no longer frantic,
a perfect way to conclude,

a lovely spring day, air crisp
with fragrant hues that play,
dancing cross meadows nigh -
    a promise to eventually mend
that rent from color to gray,

and the sense of spring is semantic
regardless, we can easily conclude,
that resurgence is not pedantic,
and we return renewed!

it falls apart

returned renewed
only to be thrown into chaos,
our absence has bred contempt
and our glory has gone apart,
unrest has brewed,
and our non-presence now an albatross
around the neck of any attempt
to regain our footing, restart.

so, renewed as we are,
we must now seek refuge,
separate ourselves from the traps
of chaos and contempt we find
ourselves, embroiled within,
an all embracing deluge,
of plots and plans, no gaps,
we find we are now resigned,

let the angels guide and protect
us in our times of turmoil and temptation.
let the cosmos steer us to act
in compassion against those that roil
against us here, let we, not fall apart!

hills of michigan

magnificent of form, face, and body you are,
i believe with my heart, that you are the star
that colors the night of these michigan hills,
causing sleepless hours - an accumulation of thrills,

but, no matter how deep, and no matter how far,
no matter the yearnings for possibilities are,
you and i can never be, for i love another
and when she married me,
i promised faith, and i promised trust,
i cannot falter, i know that i must,
remain true to myself, and true to her too,
for such is the hold golden rings have on you,

although your promise of love and life too
colors these magnificent michigan hills,
with heavy heart, and this pain in my chest
i watch as seattle bound you travel west,
while i sit alone in these michigan hills,
blue in my heart, the ache in me chills
darkens my return the city
where lies my heart
i belong to another and i always will.

nostalgia

    this bittersweet longing for <u>that</u> person,
           the wistful yearning,
                a longing for home & family;
behind this sentimental recollection lies
            a growing inequality;
treasure this feeling,
for different reasons,
            watch those tears, eyes
            whose tenderness assures
a guaranteed pay off;
for it's largely enjoyable, these reminiscences,
but painful nonetheless;
this wistfulness, what sent me on
            this short and surely frightful
            search for the original
feelings, the love, the desire,
a treasured memory to hold
during these times.

too far

been gone -- & home seems far, too far,
from here,   a faint image
colored rose from a distance,   too far.

and there my love - gazing west toward
my searching,   easterly longing,
clearly sharing the sense of loss,   too long.

egregiously flaunted - my self-imposed
laissez-faire attitude,   a faint resemblance
to the truth of needed presence, too much.

must return - home before the longing
overwhelms,   & the want & desire of
loving arms & special kisses
                 evaporate from memory
too soon.

Sentiments

avant-garde and kitsch

avant-garde - *experimental, innovative and*
unconventional;
kitsch - *showing bad taste, done in a way at once*
attractive or funny,
but thought silly, full of sentimentality &
tastelessness,
ostentatious art; Greenberg's oeuvre,
passion constantly in search of one thing --
the absolute; a search for that object
free from imperfection; complete;
an exploration that arrived at the abstract,
the non-objective art -- this poetry, too;
subject of the artist trying to imitate God,
creating validity, from the non-valid blank,
for a landscape -- not its image --
is aesthetically valid, is something given,
increate, independent of
meanings, nor similars, nor originals,
but then, of social and historical context,
consistent thru inconsistency.

lawrence

face away, learned cockatoo,
for you are we - perched upon the soul,
yes - 'tis us facing away,
   yet perched;
part of the image,
   yet not the point;

awkward, yes,
we wonder why,
   and how,
it all came to this.

part of the answer lies with
<u>the</u> lawrence, as person, as body, as celebrity,
for to look at her—on some level -
   and she needs us to -
must be as <u>she</u> specifies,
   who has the power?
   who is the law?
jlaw!

mankind

   perfectly suited
         for grand gestures;
   perfectly capable
         of grandiose things;
   a profundity of prominence
      that lies, often
           hidden, disguised as
      immodest statements
      of weighty truth,
      yet mousey little
         tidbits in the
               universal bigness -
mankind; one giant leap away
     from
         everything!

cumberbatch & armitage

intensity & intelligence,
extraordinarily gifted artists
vainglorious, as they could well adopt,
these young talents
  so reminiscent of giants long past
  who held up, to our collective faces,
statements to the greatness of man.

hawkings, van gogh, holmes, turing,
  gods waltzing among men,
    powerful physical existence
    in one sense, yet
    beyond reality in another,
simple wonderment, sharing cosmotic visions
  with we mere mortals, artist portraying
artisan & genius - dancing with exuberant joy
on the silver screens - no matter the size -
in our minds, a verifiable paradigm;
standring, guy of gisborne, monet, thorin,
  troubled anguish wrapped in
ambition, momentous passions, hiding true
    passion & compassion,
      somehow piteous in our
eyes and reason, so deserving of our
hatred & dread,
so impassioned, our leader, our force for rightness
  and sight; an impression - yes,
on our minds, hearts, & souls,
perfect power in portrayal, honor bound;

Sentiments

as laughton before, so go these
young knights, to charge our imaginations,
        portray our masters,
            our gods of men, to salute
                  with might, the best
among us,
to remind us of what greatness man can
achieve, how delightful our sense;
for no matter the stage, dimensions, location,
        our amazed admiration, awe,
            the pleasant puzzled surprise we
                  feel following performances
where we all breathe a sigh,
hold our collective breaths, admire
and admonish those characters that march across,

and we salute these portrayers of excellence
that allow our escape
        into and out of those other worlds!

ashley

she dances there,
this white-blonde waif,
pixie, darting through
the meadows of
my memory –
seen dashing toward me,
with loving, youthful abandon,
wrapping herself to me
tightly,
arms locked 'round
my neck,
a guileless beauty,
head resting on my shoulder,
sweetest,
softest embrace
forever stealing,
sealing my heart,
with simple ,solemn whisper –
"i love you"

i'm not paralyzed

i'm not paralyzed,
i'm just struck
by you,
dumb-founded & awe-thumped,
why?
profound question,
unknowable answer.
maybe, it's those
stems that go from
ground to heaven,
or maybe, it is the faultless
roundness of your ass,
maybe, those ideal
silken brown eyes,
or the glands that nurture
in their absolution,
maybe, as a finish page
to my incomplete novel,
or the final stroke in
my masterpiece of life,
whatever the raison d' être,
i strive for its full
annexation.

land of the dead?!

they are fertile fields, these abundant
rolling plains, peopled by memories,
images - places, time, faces,
some stacked like firewood, those faceless masses
        that teem our history,
seen, but not remarkable,
no power to hold, while others lie like cow pies,
the feces of life whose mere existence
marks the passage of evil periods,
stormy melodies that would wreak havoc,
if allowed but to replay,
storm driven waves that crescendo
        against the pillars of our days,
but, the magnificent,
those essentials that
sweep across us, as waves
        of shimmering brilliance,
who dance the sky full
        of rainbow hued wonder
with these are we rewarded,
for these are we thankful!

Sentiments

escarpment of neverland

they cavort there,
mystical wisps of those visages
        of acquaintances that
        were
but only vicarious in nature,
known only by study, reflections
of interpretation,
        as seen by others, mocked
by the principle's words,

she dances

and she dances
        amongst the tables,
           yet, the chairs often win,
and, that'll leave a mark,
      a badge of honor
        for the table warrior,
prima donna of the table ballet,
        maestro of the rhythmic,
waitress.

watch the traversal,
      where sometimes
the waltz will lose
          the delicate balance
within the obstacles
    that are no match
for the prowess, the attention
was distracted
a momentary lapse
for the queen of the tables.

the canvas

each & every
attitude of
                  "i am not artistic,"
rings of false modesty
      simply because
              we, as a group,
"paint" our canvas
      every day,
present to the world
      our masterpiece,
on display
      on exit the door
           to the public,
for morning ablations
      decorate the primary
           canvas of our lives,
us, we, them,
      paint & preen,
           primp & deodorize,
drape & polish
the canvas we present - ourselves.

at the end of the driveway

wander down
to the end of that concrete slab
    that marks your entrance
        to the world at large;
should you turn left?
shall i turn right?
should we fare straight thru?
what wonders abound at the end of that
excursion? what marvels? what dreams?
and it seems such inspirations
can only festoon into a lifetime of
golden memories to enjoy
as life winds down,
so i gaze with amazement at the end
of my driveway,
dazzled by the endless possibilities,
as the end of my driveway leads to
the world, and who knows
someday beyond.

Sentiments

nici

*do you know that in secret, i watch as you gaze
to that far distant future, awash in the haze
of a distant horizon, and the magical place
where a passion for the future begins apace,*

*and i grin as a smile runs away with your face
and i know that you've seen a bright shining space
with a prospect promising a gleaming tomorrow
awash with the assurance of no more sorrow,*

*i've seen that petulant frown that darkens your brow,
when something horrible occurs to upset the now,
but it doesn't last long, that darkening gaze
before you're bright once again, features ablaze,*

*and yes, you are goofy and a dancer so light,
with a spirit that gleams so fierce and burns so bright
and that form, that appearance, that mischievous grin,
at once a rapturous childish demeanor, one that's akin*

*to the cherubs in heaven, those angels above,
whose covenant is laid with the nurture of love,
is it any wonder that we watch & we long for.
a sighting, or meeting, which we'd never get o'er!?*

sea quest I

and i, wander
to where towering spires
    rake the soft underbelly
      of the dawning evening sky,
scratching softly as they
      rock gently on black, night tides
      tickling, as if to coax
a wondrous midnight sail.

Sea quest II

and i, down again
to gaze, through shaded eyes
  at the caps, so brutish white,
  that ride the waves,
    as so many tawny-hued surfers might,
as the waves rush headlong -
to thrash their might against the shore,

salted wind,
lashing teasingly 'cross my brow
  as i strain to gain,
    through reflected brilliance
    of mid-day sun,
sight of the white, driven sails dancing
the wind upon my azure seas,

yet i, down again
go, day following day,
  straining to watch,
    assaulting my senses with
    sands hot and burning,
beneath soles of feet, light hard against
my eyes, 'til i come to fulfillment.

Sea quest III

and i, to the sea again,
am drawn, and the romance
of moonlight in the high reaches
      of the tall sailing ships,
races the heart, temples dance in the blood,

and ...
as i down to the sea again, roam
i fall again into the clutches
      of my mistress, my source,
light in my sailing darkness,
bosom of my life, the sea!

sea quest IV

and I, down to the tall ships
        wander,
lust in my heart,
strong urge, desire
to see those towering spires rake
'cross sea blown sky, and
wistfully, i
        waiting the tide,
my ride -
        on that heaving breast,
        the ocean swell,
my search -
        for you, and
love, peace, tranquility --
out the sea again,
down to the tall ships, again, i
        -- waiting.

tomfoolery & shenanigans

oh, such inanity, behavior outside the norm,
but pure, sheer fun none-the-less,
    & lest you think that it is silliness
        in action only,
    nay, nay,
for words themselves can be wayward &
wandering,

we all enjoy a playful twist, a simple
mischievous prank, as long as
    no hurt is dealt & all is
        unadulterated fun,
    so let's,
with our tongues planted firmly in cheek,
we wag,

in high spirits, with high jinks galore,
our fake, prosthetic, hairy hands, finger
    pointing skyward, a salute of # one,
        saluting the sky gods,
    with a wink,
wink, we say - so long, and thanx for all
the fish!

you loved me once

your love surrounds me so,
with pleasure and with pain,
and when I'm on my own, I miss them both so,
please don't take your love to somewhere I am not,
please don't take your love to where I cannot go,

'cause, yes, I know just where my pain will end
once you have been too long gone, I know,
so I beg you now on bended knee, I beg you
not to take your love, please don't go,

and yes I know, how lonely, how loveless life
will be when you are far gone from me,
so far I cannot see the image of our life before,
when love was fresh and new,
we could not bear to part for long,

and love is so dependent simply upon you,
can I ever find another love true,
or am I destined to live alone?
remember that the book of love is fleeting,
like flickering candle light is brief
if the flame has no base below,
and no life giving air above,

you loved me true, when our
book of love was young
where, oh where, did all that love go,
why can't it find its way back?
if you have the answer, please let me know!

granddad's dirt

i remember fondly, from the days of my youth
spending training time at my granddad's knee
with lessons learned and down-home truth,
homily ridden,
worries hidden,
memories as lovely as they can be;
[chorus]
black earth, turned earth,
scents of horse dung mixed and buried,
turning the soil, planting slow, unhurried,
the sensation of sweat running down my shirt,
gotta get back to my granddad's dirt;
goin' up a dirt road, to a simple country store,
where strangers were treated just like family,
we never realized we were all dirt poor,
country rich,
family rich,
memories as lovely as they can be;

[chorus]
black earth, turned earth,
scents of horse dung mixed and buried,
turning the soil, planting slow, unhurried,
the sensation of sweat running down my shirt,
gotta get back to my granddad's dirt;
chasing down crawdad's in the family creek,
picking sweet fruit straight outta the tree,
kinfolk picking and shucking the gardens peak,
berries a cannin',
beans a cannin'

Sentiments

memories as lovely as they can be;
hearken back in memory, to my golden days,
where i learned my lessons at granddad's knee,
running and laughing and climbing trees,
miss those days when i was just a squirt,
gotta get back to my granddad's dirt!

Abstract
the tenor of image

The following are some selected images, and their matching poems, from my new book, a collection of artwork with matching poetry entitled: "the tenor of image."

sweet

a whirl –
a swirl –
a dance 'twixt
       paint
             and ash,
to twirl within -
without;
leitmotiv -
primary
       red, yellow,
       blue & green
            hidden 'neath
ashen shadow;
a gleam -
a glint –
secrets tied
       to shape & form,
stories, whose meaning
       [is] un-foretold,
simply waiting for
           discovery!

Sentiments

fan dance – an abstraction

a rose, by any other color,
would still dance
    with wavelets & droplets
      of fantasy,   *fancy*
colors that blend &
           bleed,
then tease
    an image for consideration,
    contemplation,
    pleasure –
a taste shared by many –
favored by some,
loved by several,
treasured by one,
or, just maybe, three or so,
but
        whose to know
'cept the rose and the
    prancing –
    caressing –
    preening –
    careening –
precious droplets that share!

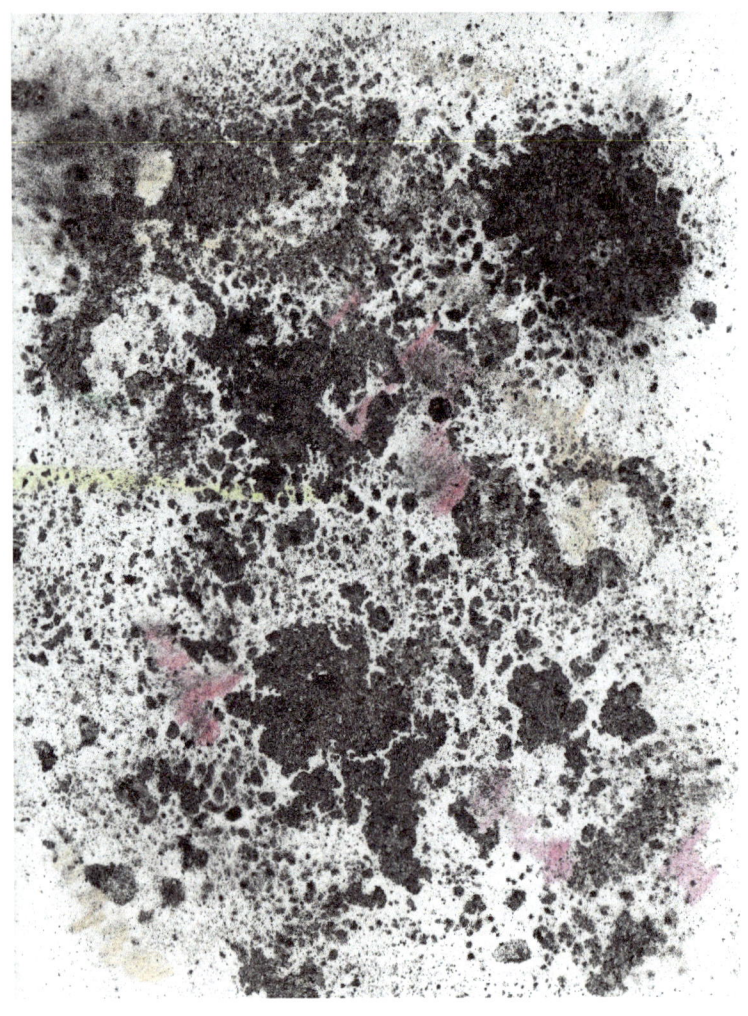

Sentiments

smoke, no mirrors – an interpretation

yeah –
lots of puffs, smoke
o   *bscuring*
                slashes & dashes,
colors peeking thru
        to tease, promises
of wonders   *hidden*
     so
          smoke, but no mirrors!

yeah –
those dots and swirls
o   *bscuring*
                image & sights,
colors adding texture
          messages? meanings?
maybe,   *but probably not,*
just
       smoke, but no mirrors!

optical haiku

*stick man walking, snowy
background, yellow accents speak;
are the ghost men dead?*

*did you see them, the
hidden rose, the gray traces; are
they simply shadows?*

*are they merely an
optical illusion, or
translation of mind?*

metallica

with sandman ringing
thru tired mind,
closed eyes swirl with
metallic colours –

drifting, sleeping wand
throws dream-state sands
that flicker with movement;
sounds drive imagery,

swirling delights – flashing
eyes, midst twirling
pinwheels; the hidden geckos
among golden traps, copper

high-lites forming smiling
faces; mystic images,
metaphors of unknown basis,
indeterminate meaning abounds

in those silvery ties that
bind all and sundry
to the promised oblivion of
healing sleep.

ink blots

swirls, & squiggles;
    lines &circles & curlicues,
        oh my!

what do you see?
    does a form catch
        your eye?

what do you sense?
    does an image turn
        your mind?

what history revealed?
what word?
what memory?

Rorschach in color,
    formless, yet moment,
        Jungian? Freudian?

or simply tint on paper?
just inkblots!

lovers?

*lovers? bound to one another
in color and form?
do you see them? do they dance
before your eyes?
or does your eye form other meaning,
other shapes, other feelings?*

*— is this
point of view exotic, outlandish
or strangely familiar?*

*is your interpretation historic,
or modern;
ancient, full of history, or*

*contemporary; old-fashioned or
progressive,   an avant   —   garde
reflection of self?*

*strange how simple mixture of
form and colour causes such
wonderment and thought!*

garden of the mind

at rest, contented
gazing thru the memories
recent – sharp,
older, hidden in mists of time
accords one perspective –
a wistful sense of longing,
of detachment;
for no matter how thorny,
how sharp the pain, or
                    vivid the ache
                    once seemed
the cooler, hazy wisps of time
    have dulled, faded, and colored
    the reminiscences;
yet, while edges and distance
    blur indistinguishable,
young, vibrant,
alive are those
    still fresh and flowing, carrying
    with them taint from the past
    and cherished hope for
                  the future;
the garden of my mind!

Abstract
In Memoriam - 2014 Part 1

The following are some selected poems from a series of collections being developed for salutes to the celebrities loved and lost during the first half of 2014. There will be follow on volumes for 2014 Part 2 and 2015 Parts 1 & 2. I hope you recognize and enjoy my reflections on these individuals.

Phil Everly

Born: January 19, 1939 - Chicago, IL
Died: Jan. 3, 2014 - Burbank, CA
Age: 74

One half of country-rock duo The Everly Brothers, the singer became famous for his guitar moves and harmonic voice. He was a noted song writer, performer, and lyricist. He had been preceded in death by his Mother & Father, the duo's first performing family, and survived by his brother "Don." The duo was elected to the Rock and Roll Hall of Fame in 1986 and the Country Music Hall of Fame in 2001.

the song fades away

aquarians alike fell silent with
grief
as one of our own, passed
and left us feeling a little more empty,
              a little more vacant,
as memories flood our senses,
and we share this grief, wonder,
and reminiscence, with all whose life was touched
by the sights, sounds, and lyrical intonations,
          and we wring our collective hearts
for the remembered past, a longing for
          those times long gone,
and we wish, but as we do
the song we so fondly bear in mind
fades away to the point of
            lyrical buzz!

wake up, little susie

"wake up, little susie, wake up,
we've both been sound asleep,
wake up, little susie, and weep,
the movie's over, it's four o'clock,
and we're in trouble deep."

and as those words echo in our minds ear,
our mind is flooded with lyrics that
said bye to love, taught us how to dream, told us
that johnny was a bird [dog], and a joker,
and made us feel for cathy's clown, a
relatable feeling for many a young man
in days past, and made us ask for
a timeline for love.

so maybe we should all say, "wake up,"
keep the memories alive, sing the old songs,
      let not the song die with the artist
for the surest way to honor them
is celebration!

... & did we pass?

celebrity and wealth, success and circumstance
did not deter service, Semper Fi say we
as did he,
        Semper Fidelis, always faithful,
a tone for life, for even though separate,
always together

until the end, derisive over politic
and life, estranged, a difficult life
together,
        but magic in music,
and we ask, are we as a whole
different?

and if we could, would we pass
any test - in music, in life, in family?
we are no different
        - so we identify, we forgive,
we accept and listen, fondly remember
and celebrate!

Philip Seymour Hoffman

Born: July 23, 1967 - Fairport, NY
Died: February 3, 2014 - Manhattan, NY
Age: 46

An Oscar nominated actor and winner (for portraying Truman Capote), Hoffman was widely regarded as one of the world's finest actors. As an actor extraordinaire, he was better at making you feel sympathy for failures, degenerates, sad sacks and hangdogs even as he played them warts and all. The New York-born actor died of a drug overdose in his apartment, where officials found envelopes of what was believed to contain heroin.

acclaimed, but troubled

many faceted, accomplished as
actor, producer, director,
theater & film oeuvres,
a growing master of all,

fearless playing reprehensible characters,
typically lowlifes, bullies, and misfits,
masterful as unmoraled villain,
slyly witty as storm chaser, &
consciously aware of all the steps
between, as actor - mounting influence;

capote's doppelganger,
brutally frank spy,
pedophilic priest &
charismatic leader - all in his
acting bag of tricks;

acclaimed as theater actor,
director & producer,
award nominated, fearless,
ambitious, widely recognized, tragic,
all terms to mark a remarkable talent,
a remarkable life!

actor of depth

a young adult, struggling with drug addiction,
sobriety lost in later life, and relapse fostered
an unexpected event widely lamented
by fans both within and without the film
and theater fraternities.

no one better at making you feel sympathy
feel those poor souls with torments,
fearlessly portrayed with the worst of qualities
front and center, warts and all.

unafraid, with a range all-encompassing,
breathing life into any role, add heft to art films, nuance
& unpredictability
to blockbuster franchises,
transformative, a performer working inside out.

blessed with emotional transparency.
at once   overwhelming,
invigorating,
*   compelling, and devastating,*
could anyone do terminal uncertainty better?
in the simplest of answers,   not in our lifetime,
and like the day the music died,
frozen february once again claimed a light,
a brilliant, blazing, soaring magic from
film and theater, and worst of all,
from our consciousness.

Maya Angelou

Born: April 4, 1928- St. Louis, MO
Died: May 28, 2014 - Winston-Salem, NC
Age: 86

The African-American author, poet, dancer, actress and singer was best known for her series of seven autobiographies, which focused on her experiences in childhood and early adulthood. Her first book, I Know Why the Caged Bird Sings (1969), brought her global acclaim. On January 20, 1993, at the first inauguration of President Bill Clinton, she read her poem "On the Pulse of Morning," becoming the second poet in history to read a poem at a presidential inauguration.

maya

acclaimed;
poet, storyteller, activist, autobiographer &
a singer, a dancer, first female black director,
    an actress and composer,
     first female and black street car
conductor,
best & most - writer, essayist,
playwright, and poet,
raising the moral standards of living
by reliving her life in word;
from nightclub shake dancer to hamburger fry cook,
from Creole dinner cook to stripping paint off cars,
lover of language,
un-frightened, un-abashed, un-ashamed,
    voice of a race,   human;
a people   American;
make the living word, bigger, richer, finer,
   more inclusive,
hero, role model,   inspiration,
celebrated spirit of St. Louis,
the phenomenal woman?
no, but as special as any
   having walked this Earth,
   shared air & sense & faith,
muse for us all!

maya, too

lost;
a voice giant across generations,
but only lost to the here & now
for her voice will echo   down the generations
rattle & toss along   the timeline
to mold & shape anew as each new mind discovers
the word
the wisdom,
the heart, the passion
     and will apply the teaching to self
         & sibling,
         to parent
         & guardian,
so to that end,
the voice shall remain   timeless,
inspirational,
motivational,
apply the voice, let it help to foster, to prop,
to aid,
for we shall not see it's like, again!

gone, but not

she left this mortal coil,
no loss of acuity,
no loss in comprehension,
a masterful mind   still masterful
to the end,
and we shall miss her quick wit, her dancing mind,
her love of life and all that it contained,
for one that lived as did she,
what marvels still lie beyond?
can we hope to meet her once again,
in another plane, in another life?
who's to say, but it burns the mind to
think that such a mind as this
should ever be lost,
gone, forgotten,
gone, but not!

About the Author

c a gallagher (nee Scott - surname) was born in Portland, ME, to an Irish Mother and an Italian-Scotch Irish Father. He spent the 1st 12 years of his life in the NE (ME-MA-NY-PA), the second 12 years in FL, & plied most of the US and parts of the world the rest of his life.

He currently resides in Nevada & Indiana, with part-time stops in Ohio & Illinois with his muse - his beautiful wife, Jacqueline, one of their daughters & a new baby grandson.

Watch for the new literary works from c a gallagher on sale now or in the near future at your favorite book retailer.

Poetry:
Subtle Ties
In Memoriam - 2014, Part1
In Memoriam - 2014, Part2
In Memoriam - 2015, Part1
the tenor of image

Fiction - as c a gallagher:
Seat of Evil
Shade

Fiction - as Rayne Storm:
Under the Aloysius Strange Sagas
Strange Mokitas
Strange Harvest
(many more to come...)

Fiction/Non-Fiction - as Crispen Scott:
Lecagy
eMail, eNet, eHome --- eGad
As Contributing Author --- Out of Print (from Que)
Running the Perfect Web-site in Windows (formerly NY)
Running the Perfect Web-site in Apache
Using CGI

Science Fiction - as Ray Gunn:
Triple Threatt
REclaim

www.ingramcontent.com/pod-product-compliance
Lightning Source LLC
Chambersburg PA
CBHW042315150426
43201CB00001B/5